AWAKENINGS

SUFI VERSE

Novid Shaid

ISBN-13:978-0993044885

DEDICATION

To the souls of: Dhun Nun Al Misri, Rabia Al Adawiyya, Shaykh Al Akbar Ibn Al Arabi, Al Ghawth Abu Madyan, Shaykh Umar Ibn Al Farid, Imam Abul Hasan Ash Shadhili, Mawlana Jalal Ud Din Rumi, Baba Bulleh Shah, Daata Saab Ali Al Hujwiri, Shaykh Abdul Ghani Al Nablusi, Shaykh Ahmed Al Alawi, Shaykh Muhammad Ibn Al Habib, Shaykh Abdul Qadir Al Himsi, Emir Abdul Qadir Al Jazairi, Shaykh Abdul Rahman Ash Shaghouri, Shaykh Nuh Ha Mim Keller, Sidi Abdal Hayy Moore, William Shakespeare, William Wordsworth, Samuel Taylor Coleridge, William Blake, John Keats, William Butler Yeats, Edgar Allan Poe, T S Eliot, Ezra Pound, Tatumkulu Afrika, Wilfred Owen, Seamus Heaney and Dylan Thomas

Human beings are asleep.
When they die, they wake up.

This saying is attributed to
Imam Ali Ibn Ali Talib
May Allah ennoble his countenance

CONTENTS

Preface

I wrote these poems because of a compelling urge which impels me to put pen to paper- feeling awake. Being awake in the realm of spirituality is when an individual rises up from his or her egotistical dreams and nightmares and suddenly witnesses the real world of the spirit.

I feel that whenever a writer or a poet has something powerful to say it is to do with that feeling of being awake, of rising up. When we really wake up, it is like finally coming home after roaming for ages, or being drowned in a sea without a shore, or witnessing some clarity after being in the dark or joining the One that you love deep in your heart of hearts.

I hope that all who read these poems can begin to appreciate this feeling of being awake and how it feels for a Muslim to gaze at the real world of Allah Most High before drifting back into sleep.

May Allah Most High grant us all wakefulness in its truest sense! Ameen

Novid Shaid, 2016

Arise my friend!
And contemplate the Real World
For I need your help as time is running out
If I have no companion here to help me,
My eyes will close
Then sleep will cast me out.
Arise dear heart! And see who truly lives
Behold the Real One illuminating everything
If we rise up together as true seekers
We can rouse ourselves when sleep comes lingering.
Stand up you subtle soul!
And observe the world's true nature
Witness the universe, just a floating speck of dust
Bask in the Blessed Light, that gives it all a meaning
Wake from the nightmare of your self and of your lusts.
Rub your eyes, dear friend!
And stretch out your horizons,
And let's link arms and sing for the One who only lives
As partners let us search for that special healer
Who will prescribe a pill which keeps us ever attentive.
Wake up my friend!
For life is rapidly passing,
And though we are engrossed,
We are but sleepwalking in a dream
Rise up and be engulfed by the One and Only
Arise and realise that we exist through Him.

The Homecoming of My Old Friend

One day, a painful memory shook my heart,
My old friend had served me since my birth,
And I had cast him out onto the street,
Denying his undying faithfulness.
For my old friend was becoming wearisome,
Especially now I'd made new, trendy friends,
In these progressing times he seemed passé,
My friends would snigger at my companion.
So, I barged him out onto the lonely street
I slammed the door as he began reasoning,
I convinced myself he was an inconvenience,
I assured my friends I had forsaken him.
Many days and weeks passed gradually,
I felt the world vibrating at my feet,
His knocking had halted some time ago,
But still I knew he lingered there, outside.
So I threw off all my guilt and held my breath,
Then leapt into the mires of my desires.
I plunged in hordes of feigned relationships,
I hosted great, extravagant soirees,
Fleeting ecstasies were my preoccupations,
My house bulged with gatecrashers gushing in,
My heart sagged with intruders surging in.
Until one day, as I jigged around my room,
Encircled by my artificial friends,
They closed in on me, stifling my breast,
They pressured me to offer them my heart,
When a slow knock rocked against my door
Its reverberation left a thunderous roar,
My body trembled like a shaken leaf
From deep within arose familiarity,
I staggered to and fro, shielding my ears,
But still the knocks resounded, thundering.

And then the realisation struck me down,
My abandoned friend was waiting in the cold.
And as this certainty aroused my heart,
Tears of shame ran, searing my desires,
Each drop fell, and my heart was up in flames,
The intruders fled, shrieking in agony.
I moved towards the knocking on my door
The tense smiles of my friends stood in the way,
Attempting to divert my attention,
They promised untold pleasure if I stayed,
But when they realised I was intent
They grabbed my legs and fought to drag me back
Their wailed and cried revealing their dismay,
And I just kicked them off with bitterness.
And so I stood there, facing my front door
I turned and saw my friends gaping in horror,
I turned the handle with my quivering hand
My heart lamented as the door opened,
I dreaded facing him after so long,
I planned I'd throw myself before his feet,
When suddenly every single thing vanished
My house, my friends, myself
And nothing else remained.
And then I found myself not in my room
But on the lonely street, there, shivering
Before me stood a great, glistening door
It opened and my old friend emerged,
He covered me with warm, comforting robes
He wrapped me in His unifying glow,
He sheltered me from sorrow and the cold,
And I had been a homeless, wretched soul,
And by His love I'd finally returned home.

Are You Lonesome Tonight?

Are you lonesome tonight?
Are you friendless tonight?
Is your world fractured apart?
Has your love turned and fled?
Has your loyal heart bled?
It's not worth living, apart.
Shall I show you a friend?
Recommend you a friend?
Your woes, His love will consume
And His veil He will rend,
And His charms have no end,
His warmth will comfort your gloom.
Are you troubled tonight?
Agitated tonight?
Have dreams been shattered and strewn?
Has your health turned to dread?
Is your wealth torn into shreds?
And you sense your impending doom.
Will you welcome a friend?
Acquiesce to a friend?
Who'll mend and replace your dreams,
And He'll freshen your health,
And enliven your wealth,
His aid will thrill your esteem.
Are you shaking tonight?
Are you aching tonight?
Without a morsel or bed?
And the cold grips your skin,
And the hunger within,
No luck or hope lies ahead.
Can you search for a friend?
Can you feel for a friend?

Who dwells in no time or place,
And His nearness will sate,
And His grace compensate,
Your fare, beholding His face.
Well then, long with your heart,
And kindle in your heart,
The wish to witness His face,
And pledge to Him your love,
Then purge for Him your love,
Your cravings don't leave a trace.
And convey peace tonight,
And then blessings tonight
Upon His dearest comrade,
And upon his close friends,
Family, companions,
Until there's no night or day.

Before

Before, I thought it all a hopeless mess
Imagined all a helpless cry of distress
Considered all a hapless guess
Rejected all a heartless process
Abandoned all, a homeless essence
Until I found it *All a h*idden blessing
Discovered *All a h*opeful beginning
Accepted *All a h*istory of genesis
Unveiled to *All a h*eavenly gnosis

When You're With Me

When I'm feeling
There's no escape
Hidden doors appear
When You're with me.

When my head's filled
With all the mess
It all clears away
When You're with me.

When You're with me
Time is still
And my old fears
Just relinquish.

I implore You
With this request
As I stumble in the dark
Be there with me.

When no other
Sees my grief
I can face the pain
When You're with me.

When I'm stumbling
On course to fail
Courage lifts me up
When You're with me

When You're with me
There's no fear

And my demons
Just disappear.

I implore You
Up to the end
As I stumble in the dark
Be there with me

When I'm sensing
The time is near
Let me see Your face
Be there with me

When I'm facing
My ugliness
Veil me with Your grace
Be there with me

If my glance steers
Away from You
Inattentive
Forgetting You

Bear my weakness
There's none but You
As I stumble in the dark
Be there with me

Where Did You Go Last Night?

He arose with gleaming eyes and the traces of last night
Still smouldering from the ardour of the tryst.
From her side of the bed, she sat up, carefully observing
Pangs of suspicion swelling, sensing some foreboding:
"Where did you go last night? Why came you home so late?"
Then like a hawk she scanned for clues upon his face.
But he just sighed so sweetly and smiled forever.
"Well?" She replied, her fears making her shiver.
He said: "after all this time I finally met Her."
"Her!" she cried, "I should have known better!"
And then her hands fixed round his neck like a pair of fetters.
"Who is she? What's the name of this strumpet!?"
Just audible he gasped: "some call Her Layla, but She's not a
harlot."
She dug her nails deeper into his neck:
"How many nights this floozy have you met?!"
He winced and said: "last night was our first meeting."
"And this morning I will inflict upon you an almighty beating!"
Shaking him like a rag doll she screamed: "what is she like?"
He coughed out: "none can compare to Her delights."
Enraged, she roared: "where does this minx live?!"
"You'll never find Her with your five senses."
She sat, head in her hands, broken and tearful:
"Why did you this to me for I was ever faithful?!"
And sobbing like a wretch she dashed into the street.
He just sat there, feeling the winds of love so sweet.
But though the Beloved One had brought him so near,
As the hours passed he began to fear
For his wife, because deep down he really did love her
She was his trusted friend, his partner, his succour.
The night closed in, his heart filled with regret:
"My love for You has chased away my dear pet!"

And through the night he couldn't taste any sleep
He was overcome with worry and raw grief.
Then as the dawn broke clear and light shone far and wide
She appeared in the doorway, with the deepest, piercing eyes.
He started up: "where did you go last night? Where in heaven!?"
To his joy, she said: "well, you see, I finally met Him!

What Do You Sing With A Drunken Dervish?

What do you sing with a drunken dervish?
Sing and cry with a drunken dervish?
What do you cheer with a drunken dervish?
Early in the morning!

Hayy! Hu! Up he rises!
Hayy! Hu! Up he rises!
Hayy! Hu! Up he rises!
Early in the morning!

Look at the eyes of a drunken dervish!
Feel the smile of a drunken dervish!
Drown in the light of a drunken dervish!
Dazzling eyes in the morning!

Hayy! Hu! Up he rises!
Hayy! Hu! Up he rises!
Hayy! Hu! Up he rises!
Dazzling eyes in the morning!

Deeper than the sea is a drunken dervish!
Brighter than the sun is a drunken dervish!
Sweeter than wine is a drunken dervish!
Gleaming eyes in the morning!

Hayy! Hu! Up he rises!
Hayy! Hu! Up he rises!
Hayy! Hu! Up he rises!
Gleaming eyes in the morning!

What do you feel with a drunken dervish?
What do you see with a drunken dervish?

What do you find with a drunken dervish?
Ecstasy in the morning!

Hayy! Hu! Up he rises!
Hayy! Hu! Up he rises!
Hayy! Hu! Up he rises!
Ecstasy in the morning!

What is the trick of a drunken dervish?
High as a kite is a drunken dervish!
Inward pure bliss outward stillness!
Sober eyes in the morning!

Hayy! Hu! Up he rises!
Hayy! Hu! Up he rises!
Hayy! Hu! Up he rises!
Sober eyes in the morning!

Deceiving to the eye is a drunken dervish!
Calm, serene is a drunken dervish!
When we're asleep he's smitten by a dear Friend
Loving eyes in the morning!

With a rock and a bow and a welcome hand!
And a pounding breath like a drummer band!
And a secret deep as the desert sands!
Profound eyes in the morning!!!

Hayy! Hu! Up he rises!
Hayy! Hu! Up he rises!
Hayy! Hu! Up he rises!
Far eyes in the morning!

Fear

A dedication to Shaykh Muhammad Ibn Al Habib, Allah sanctify his secret

If you gaze at this world with your spirit,
You'll see the light that shines through Him
If you pierce through the earth with your secret
There's naught to fear or to grieve.

When you lay in bed at night
And the dark smothered your face
A dread swelled up deep within
Then it surged up through your breast
And it choked your cries for help
Whispering: "I am your fear, loneliness"

If you gaze at this world with your spirit,
You'll see the light that shines through Him
If you pierce through the earth with your secret
There's naught to fear or to grieve.

Did you ever ask your self
Who that voice was deep inside
That would haunt your wildest dreams?
Having all the world's desires
Many friends, intoxicating fame
But it is said: "all is in vain."

If you gaze at this world with your spirit,
You'll see the light that shines through Him
If you pierce through the earth with your secret
There's naught to fear or to grieve.

Being poor and destitute
Not a penny to your name
And you cried cursing the skies,
Still that murmur in your heart
Told you search deep in your self
And you'll see there's nothing to fear

If you gaze at this world with your spirit,
You'll see the light that shines through Him
If you pierce through the earth with your secret
There's naught to fear or to grieve.

Then upon that fateful day
When you stood and faced yourself
And you turned your back from otherness
Then He raised you from yourself
Not a trace of you remained
The One Entity was all that was there

If you gaze at this world with your spirit,
You'll see the light that shines through Him
If you pierce through the earth with your secret
There's naught to fear or to grieve

Murshid

Manifesting lights of infinity
Undertaking quests of profundity
Resonating with Divine symphony
Synthesising law and subtle mystery
Honouring the rich and poor equally
Instilling disciples with deep certainty
Disguising majesty with humility

If

If you can unmask the masquerade
Of life and its illusions
then you have overcome, in truth,
all obstacles of existence.

If you can see the light of God
shimmering through every moment
there's no-one that can equal you
in this entire existence.

If others sit wrapped in their minds
ensnared by their devices
and you sit free and face your Lord
you've triumphed over all existence.

If you can push aside the noise
of people and their distractions
and see your Lord through their demands
you've conquered all existence.

If you can find, when calamities
spin through your life like whirlwinds,
the pre-eternal light of God,
you're a gem of this existence.

If you can find infinite stillness
when people around run riot
and find the One who truly lives
you've uncovered the secret of existence.

If you can face your death with peace
and recognize your frailty

then you become the triumphant one
of life and this existence.

If you can purge your heart of love
for fame and notoriety
and prefer to seek the light of God
you're elevated over all existence.

If you can make your goals for Him
and act with true intentions
the world bends, bowing at your feet
you're the master of existence.

If you can make your heart a slave
to Him, while others imagine
they're masters of their own destinies,
He makes you King of all existence.

O Lord when this world overcomes
our minds and our motivations
make us discern Your Reality
encompassing all existence

And peace be on the messenger
and blessings without concession
who, if we ever met him now,
would revive our whole existence.

The Lover, the Birdsong and the Mythical Origins of Inshaad

Once there lived a lover from Baghdad
Who loved God so much it nearly turned him mad
If he did not settle his nerves quite soon
He would disintegrate into a fiery pool.

So he roamed the Baghdad streets until nightfall
The fire of love burning stronger than a fireball
He had to find some respite from his illuminations
A channel for relieving and expressing his elation.

It just so happened that this lover had a voice
So loud and free it made all around him rejoice
But he needed inspiration, not being a trained singer
He yearned to sing for God with beautiful style and vigour.

His search went on, the yearning intolerably bad
When one dawn he noticed the birdsong of Baghdad
And at this moment Love inspired him with love
It was the moment he'd been dreaming of.

While sitting by the banks of the flowing Tigris
He sat among some trees as the sun was rising
Suddenly this lover's heart was tremendously lifted
Birdsong consumed the air, while along the Tigris drifted.

He saw a crested lark, migrating from Sheraz
Perched upon a branch singing with gravitas
The lover listened enrapt and spellbound
Imitating its melody he called it Nahawand.

Then singing for an absent friend or lover,

He heard a sighing Bul-Bul hailing from Basra
Its melancholic song echoed with the pain of separation
He called this one Saba and wept with trepidation.

A House Martin caught the lover's gaze thereafter
Singing about the haunting mystery of the holy Kaaba
He felt the fear of God, prostrating as
he listened to the bird, its song he called Hijaz.

Some cheer descended which made the lover glad
Some chirping blackbirds from the forests of Jilan
Their rousing song put the lover's heart at ease,
He called their song Bayat, Rasd and Ajami.

Then just before the lover ventured off
He heard a bird exulting in the glory of God
This swift from Nishapur, was on a journey, a true seeker
Inspired by its exultation he called its song Seeka.

And now with birdsong swirling round his head
The lover arose and saluted the birds of Baghdad
He sang their modes through days and through nights
And the people listened, imitating, lost in delight.

The Wine of Unity

For Shaykh Ahmad Al Alawi, Allah sanctify his secret

Gaze with your heart and see
A never-ending sea
Its water is the wine of Unity.
To set this secret free,
You need to turn a key
Unlock your door gaze at Eternity.
Freedom asks for a fee
Its price, none disagree,
A heart refined of all impurities.
From worldly torments flee,
Embrace Reality
Worry not of insecurity.
Ignore your ego's plea
And Shaitan's base decree,
By striving you will find security.
Leave your vulgarity,
And immaturity,
Hold firm your reins with honest dignity
With fate, be like a tree
Whether full or bare, carefree,
Soak up the rain of blessed purity.
Leave Him to oversee,
He knows your life's précis,
Your meeting is no doubt a surety.
Shrink both worlds to a pea
Squash them, as if a flea,
Then vanish by His sheer proximity.
Make Him all that you see,
Shun dire duplicity,
And witness Him with great sincerity.

Plunge headfirst in the Sea,
Keep diving endlessly,
Drown in the lights of His pure entity.
Peace and blessings be
Upon the chief of all species,
And on his house and his community.

An Ode to the Mountain Men of the Caucasus

LA ILAHA ILLALLAH!
From the mountain tops of Daghestan!
LA ILAHA ILLALLAH!
To the pounding seas of the Caspian!
LA ILAHA ILLALLAH!
In the tender grips of our fair ladies!
LA ILAHA ILLALLAH!
Or the flailing fists of our enemies!
LA ILAHA ILLALLAH!
In the charm of peace or the cloud of war!
LA ILAHA ILLALLAH!
Whether thriving, rich or struggling poor!
LA ILAHA ILLALLAH!
We will die like men with our faces high!
LA ILAHA ILLALLAH!
When they face us, see their quivering eyes!
LA ILAHA ILLALLAH!
Much better to roam like a howling wolf!
LA ILAHA ILLALLAH!
Than bow and bark like pet, woof, woof!
LA ILAHA ILLALLAH!
When the thunder came, we arose like fire!
LA ILAHA ILLALLAH!
We have no fear, Allah is our desire!
LA ILAHA ILLALLAH!
We are dust off the feet of our Pir Shamyl!
LA ILAHA ILLALLAH!
Hear his rousing voice shake the mountain air!
LA ILAHA ILLALLAH!
LA ILAHA ILLALLAH!
LA ILAHA ILLALLAH!
LA ILAHA ILLALLAH!

O Muslim men rise from your gloom!
LA ILAHA ILLALLAH!
In the morning sun and the afternoon!
LA ILAHA ILLALLAH!
In the depths of night, while the weak ones snooze!
LA ILAHA ILLALLAH!
From the inner core of your Mu'min heart!
LA ILAHA ILLALLAH!
Cry the kalima and fire up your heart!
LA ILAHA ILLALLAH!
Our bold fathers sigh from their graves!
LA ILAHA ILLALLAH!
We have lost our light we have lost their way!
LA ILAHA ILLALLAH!
So unite with them as they roar with love!
LA ILAHA ILLALLAH!
Drown your heart and soul with His noorani flood!
LA ILAHA ILLALLAH!
LA ILAHA ILLALLAH!

Freedom

Musty fumes belch out
of Kabul's downtown sprawling mass
of rambling rickshaws, tooting Toyotas,
trotting horse drawn carts,
heaving and straining
with the weight of rotting carcasses
and the salvaged wreckages of time.
But she does not sigh with disgust.
Her breath is taken away.
She sways her head gently to and fro,
chadour hanging loosely
The ancient breeze of darya Kabul
blowing through her hair,
which she now absorbs, gladly,
in the throes of her freedom,
because the Talibs have been chased out of town
and the misty sun, casting its gaze,
gives her the promise of a new age
a prospect of progress,
shedding the old skin
of the worn out trends of myopic mullah men.
 She strides, confidently, past
A seated apparition on the sidewalk
who sits cross-legged on a flattened cardboard box,
living behind a worn blue, gigantic shuttlecock,
a row of chadri clones laid out before her
displayed for only 500 Afghani.
But this woman from nowhere
would make jealous even the eyes of Socrates
as she sits on her throne, the universe,
where she basks in eternal lights
which flood through her, like the rolling sea,

reducing the world around her and the cosmos
to a floating speck of dust,
which would have lived in the shadows
if the light of the One had not revealed it.
And while the winds of time and war
wreak havoc around her,
beneath her prison,
she smiles
because she has freed herself
from the shackles and cells of time and space
for she had learned to recite the Name
until the Named was all she witnessed
and now she bathes in the Sun, mesmerised,
while selling her clothes, seeing to her brood,
putting up with her poor excuse for a life,
gazing, unfettered and unrestrained,
at the haunting beauty of His Face.

An Ode to the Hadra

Plunging through the seas
Drowning all who join
The Hadra sets them free

Everlasting Lights!
Surround them and unite!

Linking palms attract
Meanings interact
Inner essences
Expand and then contract

Intoxicating Lights!
Mesmerising, Infinite!

Lovers sing the odes,
Murid hearts aglow
The Hadra resonates,
Their inner doubts implode.

Liberating Lights!
Releasing through the night!

Seekers ride the waves
Radiant and amazed,
The songs of Arifeen
Compel them, captivate.

Captivating lights!
The veils, they override!

Rocking like the sea,

Resounding endlessly,
The hadra unifies
Their spirits, by Decree.

Annihilating Lights!
Ignite hearts with true life!

Peace on him, the key
to His great mysteries
And blessings ceaselessly
And friends and family.

Alleviating Lights!
Sobering with sheer delight!

Behold With Your Heart

Behold with your heart!
His everlasting light,
Behold with your heart, behold!
Behold with your heart!
This overwhelming sight,
Behold with your heart, behold!

Beyond everything
Gazes the True King
Who fashioned all that we know.
Peerless is His might
Endless His timeless light
Find Him through your heart, behold

Chorus: Behold with your heart! (...)

He lives without sleep
He reigns without fear
His throne is without a heir
He dwells in no place
No era, no space
His light glistens everywhere

Chorus: Behold with your heart! (...)

The skies and the stars
The lands and the seas
Are nothing other than signs,
Each atom there is
Signals the Unity
That encompasses everything

Chorus: Behold with your heart! (…)

The Drops of Purity

The limpid drops of purity
Seep through their hearts instilling certainty.
They rain down on the turbidity,
Which veils their hearts with all things sensory,
And soften the solidity,
And wash away the multiplicity.
The drops increase and permeate
A vision forms in the transparency,
It's like the rising of the Sun
The lights glisten and dance in harmony.
The dust has cleared; the sight is free
The lights engulf them, veiling their identities,
The clearing shows Infinity
The Endless Light revealing endlessly
There's nothing in reality
Except the One and Only entity
And all besides is illusory
A picture formed with perfect artistry
Appearing real, diverse, 3D
Behind these sights resounds the order, Be.
All that there is, was and will be,
Are suspended in the timeless grip, hanging helplessly.
And nothing lives independently
Although some find this an absurdity.
If they considered truthfully,
And shed themselves of their complacency
Then wrapped their selves in poverty
And soaked their intellects in humility,
The rain would fall, most certainly
Drenching their hearts and revealing His Divine Unity.
If people find some clarity
In these words and some lucidity

Then praise the One, it's His decree
The mercy of His sheer sublimity.
But if there are extremities,
Or glaring faults and poor inaccuracies
Ignore them with a conscience free,
They come from him who composed this poetry.
And peace the number of the trees
And blessings on the Prophet of purity,
And on his house and progeny
His friends, helpers and blessed community.

He Who Never Dies

Fervent fires are raging
During freezing nights,
Restless seas are writhing
In the stillest nights,
Ardent hearts are sighing
During silent nights,
Yearning for their cherished Friend,
He, who never dies.

And His flames consumed them
Searing every whim,
And His sea rushed through them
Drowning all within,
And their hearts were stolen,
Plucked out from within,
Taken to their Friend's abode,
He, who never dies.

Every single moment
They long for their Friend,
Whether safe or stricken
They entreat their Friend,
In all circumstances
They behold their Friend,
They can never live without
He, who never dies.

In the world you'll see them
Though their hearts with Him,
Through our hearts, He gazes
Though we're unaware,
Countless peace and blessings,

On him, the most aware,
Beloved of the loving Friend,
He, who never dies.

The Rich and the Poor

A road sweeper whispered some words while clearing autumn
leaves,
which lay below the naked elms that lined a privileged street.
A tear fell from his gentle eyes, landing upon a leaf,
reviving it for just a while from separation's grief.
He brushed along past wealthy folk, dining in an eatery,
where a captivating cover girl sat smiling playfully.
She luxuriated in the spell she cast upon the men,
who could not help a lingering glance while reading their
menus.
A quantum physicist drew praise for winning the Nobel prize,
Behind him sat an oligarch, lavishing gifts on his new bride.
A stand-up comedian, top draw, left his table roaring with
laughter,
his friends hanging on every word that came from him
thereafter.
And many other members of the finest echelons
ate happily, while with the leaves the man mumbled his song:

"Were I to lose the ecstasy of being near to You
And in exchange be courted by the fairest lady of the land
Then I would be the most wretched of losers.

Were I to lose the felicity of seeing nought but You
And as a consequence be the talk of people all around,
Then I would be the most wretched of losers.

Were I to lose the timelessness of Your pure entity
And then penetrate the mysteries of space and time travel,
Then I would be the most wretched of losers.

Were I to lose the serenity of hearing nought but You,

And subsequently be the greatest orator of the times,
Then I would be the most wretched of losers.

Were I to lose Your riches and my desperate poverty
And then inherit mansions adorned with landscape gardens of
gold,
Then I would be the most wretched of losers."

The Meeting

Innamaa hadhihi hayaatu mataa' – "verily this life is full of
struggles"- Young Fata to Dhun Nun Al Misri– Kitab Ul Futuwwa
Abadan tahinnu ilaykumu arwah – "forever do the spirits find rest
with You" – Imam Shihaabudeen Suhwardi

When I was a restless youth
And my heart was searching for truth
A chance meeting transformed me
And I was born again, weeping like a baby.

It was as I roamed and strode
Through the streets, heaving in a state of overload
My head was grinding and saturated
With worldly worries and grasping faces.

And the world seemed dangerous and malicious
Talk and gazes looked so vicious
About the things that I believed
People burned my book of dreams.

Then I caught a glimpse of him
And I couldn't help but wince,
At the light which shone so bright
Right on through to a paradise.

He stood, helpless, back to the wall
surrounded by these menacing Neanderthals
who jostled, poked and sniggered,
laughing at his clumsy clothes and rough condition.

And though I was hesitant and afraid
These boys had cruelty written all over their gazes

I couldn't stop myself from saving
him, the lights pulled me in, amazing.

And when I stood before these guys,
without warning, they dematerialised.
And now I stood before his eyes.
I drowned in a sea of light, and cried.

He stood silent for a while
Handing me a cloth for my tears to dry.
Then he looked deep in my eyes
And sang to me these unforgettable lines:

"I'm a poor man on the road
I live without abode
Only scraps are good enough for me
Few desire to speak with me.

But when Your sun rose in my life
And Your moon reflects Your light
The warmth eases my pain
And pure cheer graces my days.

And when I meet Your special friends
O the joy and hope they bring
As we sing about Your light
While this aging world staggers by.

So take the rough and tumble on the chin
Fear not of people and their din
For this life is hope and fear,
The pain rides with the cheer."

Then he left and I never saw him again
But the anguish was cleared from my head.
And I saw things as they are

Lights engulfed me, spectacular.

Now I roam on through this life
With energetic children and busy wife.
Leaning on each other for motivation
Sometimes suffering the trials and tribulations.

But every now and then, we cry,
With tears of joy and heavy sighs
The lights of heaven shine and glisten
And I can't help but stop and sing:

"I'm a poor man on the road
I live without abode
Only scraps are good enough for me
Few desire to speak with me.

But when Your sun rose in my life
And Your moon reflects Your light
The warmth eases my pain
And pure cheer graces my days.

And when I meet Your special friends
O the joy and hope they bring
As we sing about Your light
While this aging world staggers by.

So take the rough and tumble on the chin
Fear not of people and their din
For this life is hope and fear,
The pain rides with the cheer."

Our Night Out

Come and join our night out on the go!
A night of light where your worries will disappear
See our smiles and happy tears that flow!
We promise you our hearts and ready ears.
First we'll perform our wudu one by one,
Ensuring every limb is wet and clean,
We'll offer two rakat before our night's begun,
Our night will open solemn and serene.
Then we'll don our caps and baggy trousers
Slapping on the best attar around!
And out we go all linking arm in arm,
Heading for our local masjid down the road.
And there we'll enter carefully, right foot first.
We'll greet the mosque with warm, honest delight.
The turbaned man will read the blessed verses,
We'll pray Allah will bless our chosen night.
Then we'll march all jolly up the town
Gathering at the famous rupture dome.
And there we'll join the raq of wild renown
Bowing, rocking, swaying while all intone.
We'll budge up close to share some rice and curry
Making sure all have a healthy share,
Sitting on our knees we needn't worry
Our stomachs settle well without a care.
And then we'll lie out in the spacious yard
Staring at the silent sparkling sky
The blessed winds brushing by like soft foulard
The hints of sunrise appearing by and by.
And homewards you'll remark our sober eyes
Although our hearts are dancing in the skies.

The Fallen

A warm shower of dignified applause
Echoes down the winding road,
As hearses bearing the fallen one,
Glide through, leaving copious tears
And stoic faces in their wake.
Mourners rush forward into the road,
Roses scatter above, gently falling away,
Poor George had his whole life before him
Until an IED sent him instantly
Into the realm of Eternity.
He'd been so keen to serve his country,
Which now stood silently as his body passed by.
High within the Hindu Kush,
Wailing women and screaming children
Shed defiant and agonising tears
As wagons cradling infant souls trot away.
And grizzled elders bury their young,
Who beat them to the grave.
Poor little Hussain did not deliberately linger
When a drone floated above, homed in,
Leaving him a martyred son
And his village burned to a cinder.
He never enlisted for any state or local renegades,
He just happened to emerge in a world
Entangled and suspended in war.
And he will not make any more choices,
For he has quaffed the chalice of Infinity,
Which makes this world seem like a cheap matinee.
Angels innumerable and holy,
Greet him as he haunts their pathways,
And entreats the One who brought him back,
Fallen so suddenly

Poetic Prayer in Response to Hadith 24, Arbaeen Nawawiyya: Ya Ibaadee

O Allah! O everlasting King!
O heirless Emperor! Oh Sovereign!
O You, who has forbidden oppression
For yourself, and outlawed transgression.
O You, without whom all become astray
Without whom, none can travel on the way
O You, who solely sates our appetites
Quenches our thirst and nourishes our insights,
O You, without whom all remain unclothed,
Without whom, our frailty lies exposed,
O You, who veils our mortifying sins,
Conceals our shame and saves us from ruin,
Conserve us from oppressing one another
Preserve us from transgressing one another
Innerve us with Your fitting gratefulness
Reserve for us Your loving gentleness
Maintain us on Your liberating road
Which reaches Your perpetual abode.
And feed us with revitalising fare
Bought with an income honourable and fair,
And wrap us in emancipating robes
Which free us of conceit and repel the cold,
And draw a clement cloak over our crimes
Shore-up our fragments with Your pillars sublime.
O fearless One! We cannot cause you harm,
O peerless One! It's You who clears our qualms.
O Lord, we state this candid affirmation
Should all the beings of Your whole creation
Be servants of the highest moral station,
They wouldn't boost Your kingdom in the slightest.
O Lord, we swear this earnest declaration

Should all the beings of Your countless nations
Be tyrants of the lowest moral station,
They wouldn't shrink Your kingdom in the slightest.
O Allah, we sing Your acclamation,
Should every soul from time's initiation
And every one to life's ordained cessation,
Ask for their wants in one, vast congregation,
And should You answer every single prayer,
And meet the needs of all that gather there,
It wouldn't drain Your bounty in the slightest.
So when our acts of righteousness are sewn,
Let us affirm Your goodness, not our own.
And when our sinful acts begin to swell
Give us the common sense to blame ourselves.
And make our repentance lasting and true,
Until we fear and love no one but You.
And peace and blessings on Your courtier
Who thrives in Your confidence without barrier.

Shade Us By Your Throne O Lord

When the Sun is two bows' length,
When the heat will not subside

Shade us by Your Throne, O Lord
Shade us by Your Throne.

On the day the Horn erupts
While the living ones devise

Shade us by Your throne O Lord,
Shade us by Your throne.

When the Trump is blown again
And the souls are unified,
On the day the Trump summons
All that are and all that were,
Naked, sweating, trembling
None can flee the summoning,

Shade us by Your throne O Lord
Shade us by Your throne.

When all stand upon the plain
And there's nowhere left to run
Not a tree to shrink behind
Not a crack to crawl into,

Shade us by Your throne O Lord
Shade us by Your throne.

When the lords and the paupers
Are standing equal side by side
When the wild and the jinn

Are still and silent by our sides,

Shade us by Your Throne O lord
Shade us by Your Throne.

When our nakedness won't shame us
As we're weighing up in vain,
Some are crawling on their bellies
Faces drag bodies along

Shade us by Your throne O Lord
Shade us by Your throne.

When the Sun is on our heads,
And the perspiration floods,
Some are drowning in their sweat
For the sins they had amassed,

Shade us by Your throne O Lord
Shade us by Your throne.

When the heavens rend asunder
Flowing silver and yellow
When the heaven's molten copper
And the mountain's carded wool

Shade us by Your throne O Lord
Shade us by Your throne.
When our mothers have renounced us
And our children won't come near
And our friends have all dispersed
As they have other pressing cares,

Shade us by Your throne O Lord
Shade us by Your Throne.

When there's no one left to turn to
When there's no-where left to run

Shade us by Your Throne O Lord
Shade us by Your Throne.

When the Sun is two bows' length
When the heat will not subside,

Shade us by Your Throne O Lord,
Shade us by Your Throne.

Hard Times Hard Truths

Can't you hear me?
Can't you see my distress?
Can't you do anything?
When will you stop all this?
When will it end?
When you will make things right?
Can't you see their pain?
Can't you hear their cries?
Can't you see they're in despair?
It's all a mess!
It's all unfair!
It's all just hypocrisy!
I need justice!
I want revenge!
Are you even there?

I can hear you,
And every word you say
And even everything you think.
I know you better than you know your self.
I know your deepest fears
And your secret ambitions.
I am never absent,
I am ever present,
I love what I made
More than you will ever know.
I need no rest,
I don't have eyes like yours,
But I am always watching and doing,
And I do as I please,
But I need no effort to act.
I do as I will,

Everything pleases My will,
Nothing can change My will,
Nothing can be done without Me.
I know the beginning,
I have already seen the end,
So none can trick Me with a lie,
And none can hide the truth from Me
The truth belongs to Me
I reveal the truth,
I know the truthful,
I know all the liars and I punish the liars
I distinguish the true from the false.
I don't need justice,
For justice is My way,
I have arisen
And I have destroyed
Every oppressor from beginning to end.
I have avenged oppression,
I have restored justice,
I have exposed hypocrisy,
I have settled all conflicts,
I have resolved every paradox,
There was never a mess,
I reveal My signs for all to see,
I reveal Myself to Myself,
But you are too short sighted to understand.
So don't lie to yourself about Me
And don't lie to Me about your self,
Seek the truth in your self,
Then you will see the truth revealed through Me.
Destroy the hypocrisy in your self,
Then you will truly live through Me.
Establish justice in your self,
Then you will see true justice through Me.
Have faith in My power,
Then I will restore you through Me.

Trust in My power,
Accept My hard truths,
Then I will protect you
I will make you timeless
in Hard times

Our Love

O You, who love to demonise
our Prophet, Nabi Muhammad,
know this:
that we love him more
than you love your own identities.

O You, who love to satirise
our master, Nabi Muhammad,
know this:
that just our eulogies of him
are enough to fill your libraries.

O You who seek to stigmatise
our leader, Nabi Muhammad,
know this:
however much you put him down
our Lord increases him in nobility.

O You who are horrified
by our devotion to Nabi Muhammad,
know this:
that he lives in our dreams
and appears before our very eyes.

O You, who love to vilify
the life of Nabi Muhammad,
know this:
that some of us shed tears
by just the mention of his memory.

O You, who love to trivialise
our mentor, Nabi Muhammad

know this:
that we instil his acts
we pay homage to his reality.

O You, who seek to criticise
our love for Nabi Muhammad,
know this:
that we are helplessly in love
indifferent to your modernity.

O You, who seek to neutralise
our love for Nabi Muhammad,
know this:
that were you to offer us immortality
just a glance of him would be our sufficiency.

O You, who will never rationalise
our love for Nabi Muhammad,
know this:
were you to wipe us off the face of the earth
our dust would drift to warm Madinah.

An Ode To My Sofa

Forgive me my dear sofa,
For my wilful arrogance,
It's only now I've noticed
Your uncanny consciousness.

Your seats are so inviting!
Your back so comforting!
We fall on you for joy and rest
And you oblige our every whim.

For sleeping you indulge us,
You accommodate our guests,
On you we share our hopes and dreams,
And our children spill their breakfast.

But one thing, my dear sofa,
That chills me to the bone,
Is that on the day when time stands still,
You will speak in an honest tone.

When I stand upon the plain,
With my history laid bare,
You will speak of everything
That I did within your care.

Every word and every thought,
Whether pleased or overwrought
On that day you will not hold back
To reveal my every act.

So now I gaze at you, a compound
Of leather and upholstery,

Sitting silently and lifeless
Weakening through maturity

But one day you will awaken
With a voice so clear and free,
When the days and nights have ended
You will reveal our history.

A Prayer: The Promised Land

O Lord,
I cling on to the rocks of your sacred path, dangling
over
the
bottomless
abyss
of
my
capricious
soul,
knowing full well I have stumbled
and lost my footing
on the firm ground of certitude and witnessing.
Truly, I have slipped
away
and fallen into disarray
since You welcomed me into
the Promised Land
Of Your nearness and knowledge.
Forgive me my dear Lord,
For I lost my focus on the centre
the kernel,
the key to everything.
Something caught my eye,
A puppet show in the supermarket of this world,
masquerading as a worthy distraction.
And I followed it,
twisting through the blessed streets and paths,
Until I found myself,
abandoned
beyond the safety of the city walls
clutching onto my shoulders,

with the mighty doors slamming in my face.
Then terrible winds thrust me in the direction of Hell;
And I suffered
feeling the remoteness from Your blessed space
exclusion from Your overflowing presence
which brings all created things into existence.
And now I struggle
hanging on to the rocks
which gives me some hope that all is not lost.
O Lord
I have truly faltered,
From resting in Your intimate home,
bathing in Your perspicacious pools
and picking the fruits of Divine secrets
in your prodigious orchards,
I find myself coughing up
the sods and dirt,
clinging on to a solitary jutting rock of hope
while the gaping chasms of my emptiness and desires
await me for their feed.
My errors have been lamentable and gross
My ingratitude unforgivable
But now I call on Your Benevolence
Greater than all the Kings that ever ruled the land and sea
Help me up again O Lord,
Give me the strength
to climb up this godforsaken precipice.
And grant me
An opportunity
to make some recompense
to plead for Your forgiveness
make me a permanent resident, O Lord
A true patriot
An established citizen
Admit me once again, O Lord,
Into Your promised land

Where one truly understands Your Loving Grace,
Where one truly realises
that nothing in this whole universe, ever,
can compensate
for the infinitely intoxicating and sobering vision
of Your Face

A Prayer of Gratitude

O You, without form
Ar Rahman, Ar Raheem
Unlike all we imagine
Free of error and need.

O Lord! As I witness this world
On the spellbinding screen
Showing pain and suffering
Worse than I could ever dream.

O Lord! As I hear of the problems
Which unsettle my soul
Of the abuse of innocence
Of the Earth's dwindling capital.

O Lord! As I wince and complain
At the blows of fate
The pressures of modern living
And the storms people create.

O Lord! As my heart brews and trembles
With foreboding and stress
A pulsation of waves
Clears my heart of the mess.

O Lord! Oh Allah!
Ar Rahman, Al Raheem!
Thank you for my life!
As a free human being!
If it were Your choosing
I could never exist
I would never have sensed
This world of consequences.

O Lord! Oh Allah!
Ar Rahman, Ar Raheem!
Thank You for the safety!
All my life, I have seen!

If it were Your choosing
I could have survived
Through the horrors of war
And terrible genocide.

Thank You for this safety
Keep me free from all harm,
Relieve those who are living
Frightened and alarmed.

O Lord! O Allah!
Ar Rahman, Ar Raheem!
Thank You for the blessing!
Of my whole family!

If it were Your choosing
I could have grown up
An orphan, so lonely
Without love or childless.

Thank You for this bounty
Of my kith and my kin.
For my mother and father
For my wife and children.

O Lord! Comfort the orphans,
And those yearning for offspring
And increase all these blessings
That I find myself in.

O Lord! O Allah!
Ar Rahman, Ar Raheem!
Thank You for the soundness
Of my body and mind!

If it were Your choosing
I could have maladies
Or my body disabled
Or my mind ill at ease.
Thank You for my health
And my consistent energy
Protect me from illness
From depression and lethargy.

Strengthen those with weakness
Spread Your mercy on the lame
Help those who are suffering
From their aches and their pains.

O Lord! O Allah!
Ar Rahman, Ar Raheem!
Thank You for employment
For the flow of money.

If it were Your choosing
I could have lived wretched
As a slave or a pauper,
Or a street-dwelling beggar.

Thank You for my job!
And my honest income.
Increase me in wealth
As much, in Your wisdom.

Help those on the streets
And those searching for means

Give me the power
To help my brothers in need.

O Lord! O Allah!
Ar Rahman, Ar Raheem!
Thank You for my food
And water, fresh and clean.

If it were Your choosing
I could have lived in arid lands.
Where water is scarce
And no food close to hand.

Bless me with clean water
Provide me with good food
Make paths for those searching
For water so cool.

Help me to consider
How great water is.
And give me the wisdom
Not to waste such a blessing.

O Lord! O Allah!
Ar Rahman, Ar Raheem!
Thank You for the warmth
In my home and the heat.
If it were Your choosing
I could be living, so cold.
In winds so inhospitable
It would rattle my bones.

Protect those who are living
In the cold and the winds
And continue to warm me
Though I stress and I sin.

O Lord! O Allah!
Ar Rahman, Ar Raheem!
Thank You for my soul,
And in You, I believe.

If it were Your choosing
I could have been blind
To the truth of Your Light
Which shines beyond time.

Bless me with true faith,
Give me a safe passage through death.
Guide those on the path,
For the truth is their quest.

O Lord! When I think
How unsettling life can be,
Just the thought of Your blessings
Cheers my heart, endlessly.
And send perfect peace
On the pure, grateful one,
And send him Your blessings,
To his family, and companions.

The Coming Storm

There's a storm brewing
beyond the horizon.
Momentary flashes of electrical impulses
flicker far ahead
like a Divine pyrotechnic display
with pulses of hypnotic lights
illuminating the earth.
From afar so mesmerising
full of promise and surprise.
But we all know
when it hangs above our heads
when the eye reigns supreme
our world could be ripped apart
and our lives may never be the same again,
until the malignant eye winks out once more
and the Sun and the warm breezes
breathe rejuvenating winds into the earth.
Should we run for cover and secure our world?
Or face, like Lear, the full fury of the storm?
Or join our brothers in repelling its thunder
and deflecting the wrath of its burning eye?
I guess it's better just to live our truth,
shaking off the haze of speculation
exiting the tunnels of vain anticipation
and when the eye overlooks our darkened skies
penetrate beyond its reach, right through the ether
and gaze into the heavenly mirrors
heeding the reflections.

The Battlefield

I battle with myself
Face to face, punch for punch,
My future launches at me in front
And my past creeps up from behind.
I dodge the assault of late night party invitations,
And avoid the ambushing memories of early mistakes:
Phone numbers of girls.

I am training myself
Readjusting my senses,
Building my defences
To fight this relentless interior jihad
Slipping bullets of gluttony
And evading grenades of pride
They fire and explore around me
But I strive to keep my ground.

Before I was a pathetic refugee
Pitching tents in dunya, surrendering.
My body was conquered by the whispers of shaitan.
Battalions of lust seduced my tempted eyes
Fleets of laziness surrounded my rafts of discipline
Guerrillas of gluttony raided my rare Ramadans.
Ducking stones of anger
And parrying the arrows of desire
My past smacks me with a mighty blow
But I recover straight away.

How I have betrayed my heart!
Robbed it of Islam
Pillaged it of worship
Starved it of prayer
But engulfed it in the oil of haram.

My heart had been hard and dead
The stench of sin wreaked in my chest
Suffocating my heart
Encrusted in sins
An impervious rock.

But now the filth is softening!
Slowly the shell is weakening!
Now the sea of Islam is eroding away
The sticky rocks of dunya.
And my heart is breathing air again
Fresh and pure air it was born to breathe!

So I am left here, armed and ready
Standing alone on the battlefield
With the opposing armies of haram and shaitan
Itching to launch a strike.
But now it is I who attack!
Piercing their armour by praying
Bending their swords by repenting
Disarming their archers by reading the Quran
Crippling their cavalry by lowering my gaze.

This war will never end
My desires will never give in
They fire and explode around me
But I strive to keep my ground.

Suffering

The screaming of my child,
As she dies of hunger and thirst,
Has destroyed my taste for life
And stuffed me full of emptiness.

My ancestral home,
Has been battered to the ground,
My tribe lay still and violated,
Scattered and strewn around.

I regard with growing disbelief
The rape of virgin villages,
And the enrichment of cityscapes,
Which strips me of my hope,
And reveals my naked despair.

Yet still my heart beats along
It can't give up the need,
Despite my unrelenting pain,
Deep down, I want to live.

I'm locked within this hopeless state,
The world around me bleeds,
Pain surrounds me like a flood,
And still I yearn to live.

Life for me once was a rose
And now I feel the thorn,
Help me to wrench it from my heart
Not suffering alone.

I've Returned to the Lord of Honour and Might

For people who have lost children

Dear Mother and Father, do not fret or fear,
For I've returned to the Lord of Honour and Might.
Although you're yearning for me with each painful tear,
Know that I've returned to the Lord of Honour and Might.
For I've returned to the Lord of Honour and Might.
He gifted me to you but now He's summoned me,
Back to the gardens with rivers of pure milk,
And fruits the like of which you have never seen.
Forgive me, my parents, for I crept away from you.
I left you, then you discovered me silent and cold.
That was just my shell, my spirits' flown away,
Forgive me, I was summoned, and I just couldn't delay,
I love you but I was summoned by my special Friend,
He has no beginning and He has no end,
His light shone through me and I saw heaven above,
I gazed at children like me dancing full of joy,
Receiving counsel from our Prophet Ibrahim,
Although I stopped and looked back at your world
I could not resist my Creator's loving hold.
So dear parents there's no use grieving until you are tired and
old,
I skip with angels, and there never is a night,
For I've returned to the Lord of Honour and Might.

Dear Mother, fear not that I should ever go hungry!
My Lord is ever bounteous and wise.
Dear Mother fear not that I should ever come to harm,
I dance in gardens guarded by dazzling lights,
I play in fields where there never casts the night,
For I've returned to the Lord of Honour and Might.

Dear Mother, now I climb up the gates of Eden,
Fear not because up here I can never fall,
I have even seen the face of My Loving Lord,
And now I shall never fear and I shall never grieve.
I await you on a day when only Prophets can intercede,
On the day when many will be slipping
Fear not, for my prayers shall never let you fall,
I praise my Lord in circles drowned in light,
I've returned to the Lord of Honour and Might.

Dear father fear not that I shall be neglected!
For now my teachers are the Prophets and the Saints,
One day I shall take you by the hand,
When the scales are lifting, while the people shiver and stand,
I shall grasp you, leading you ahead
Across the bridge which will fill humanity with dread,
I will take you to the gardens where there is no night,
I have returned to the Lord of Honour and Might.

Dear Mother and Father listen to my plea,
Don't worry, you have not heard the last of me,
I'll be expecting you in the afterlife,
Don't let this world blind you by its lights,
Prepare yourself for a place where there is no night
For my Lord is no doubt your Lord too
And He will summon every last one of you,
So smile through your tears when you think of me
I'm dancing in the gardens where there never is a night
I have returned to the Lord of Honour and Might.

Uprising

The uprising
upsurges, escalating,
preparing the ground for
a ground breaking
an earth-shattering
downfall
of the monolithic pyramids of stone
the toppling of the fearsome rock faces,
which fall down with full force,
smashing into tiny fragments,
swept away by the winds of inevitability.
A downpour of torrential hope
floods the land,
engulfing the entire planet,
then slowly seeps away through the cracks,
sinking, soaking
through the recesses of the earth,
drying up
until an army of ants,
emerges, regroups,
gathers the debris
laying the foundations
of another impressive form
in the spellbinding sands of time.
Way below,
dripping drops of hope
begin filling gaps again
gaps which will eventually fill
as the new shadows grow impressively above,
and the hope can't stand to be contained.
Rising, falling, sinking, standing,
the earth persists,

ants will be ants
and hope never desists.

World Events

Like an inexorable river, thundering
Gaining in momentum, swelling
With waves, growing and towering
Like an army of marauding giants
The multifarious events of this world
Pain and cheer, disaster and stability,
Flow unstoppably towards a gargantuan waterfall
Spraying relentlessly into the air of time.
Some drops of water plummet like weighty rocks
Crashing into our surfaces,
Shattering our cohesion and faces.
But other drops float and slide gently
Like snowflakes, resting, merging, unifying
Bringing calm, restoring unity.
Then foam rises
Forever resurrecting from the impact
Of event and reaction,
Forming convoluted clouds of discontent
Sometimes forming an arresting apparition
Which vanish, returning from whence they came.
Before we all evaporate into the ether,
Will we enlighten or touch?
Will we darken or repulse?

Using Language

Using language
is like painting pictures
and shaping sculptures
in endlessly renewable ways.
You can choose, frame and fuse;
gel, mould or place;
shape, shift, then stretch;
cast to and fro; weave below;
adjust and combine and compose;
connect or exploit or mingle;
fashion and shackle and sculpture;
shuffle around and sprinkle;
transpose, interject, integrate,
interpose, here and there, interweave;
rearrange, intersperse or reshuffle;
synthesise in a polished amalgam;
assemble as one, intermingle;
accumulate then amalgamate;
or manipulate to your own ends
words, which mutate or perpetuate;
clauses, that dictate or subordinate;
phrases which detonate or encapsulate
a universe of sound effects,
illusions, confusions and truths.
In the hands of an accomplished user,
words run like free-flowing paints
with strokes of all traceable weights,
spreading colours of every known hue,
raising tones which create shifting moods.
And each word that is utilised is
a subtle and measured brush stroke,
infusing with elating light

imbuing with pulsating life,
animating, stimulating, illuminating
the works of art:
the gallery of human life.

They Will Live On

They will live on and thrive
Dressed in the raiment of true freedom
Dwelling where they please without pain or fear
They will live on and prosper
Untouchable, undisturbed
Forever young and free, resplendent
Gazing at the beatific vision
Which sends their hearts
into a state of unimaginable bliss
Extinguishing all the memories
And the surge of marching boots
Breaking their thresholds
Barking orders, bearing down, raging eyes.
And no state or spies will ever find them
For they sought to ensnare bodies and minds
And they revelled in their power
In the fear that they inspired in the innocents
But spirits are always free
And now they live on,
For those who sought to live
Will always live on
And those who seek to stifle life
Their spirits are already dead.
Oh Lord, bless the innocents for You are ever Kind
And protect those who fear in these dangerous times.

O You

O You, who created the dazzling light of the sun,
which fills the sky at dawn
with a mesmerising crimson complexion,
and grows in height and strength until it scales its zenith
beaming down from way on high,
illuminating and majestic.

O You, who casts the lustrous light of the moon,
which pervades the night sky with a radiant attitude.
And when the moon reveals its whole blooming face,
The darkened sky displays
an image of such heavenly grace
But, alas, the lights of the sun and moon ebb and abate,
Each knowing full well, that their lights daily terminate.

O You, who composed our heavenly spheres
with Your sheer power
How strange it is that the lights
in the hearts of Your awliya,
which may be clothed in skin and cells, aging and ailing,
the lights of their hearts grow brighter,
each moment, intensifying.
The sun and moon of the sky shine bright
but are destined to fade,
While the hearts of the awliya glow
with a light that proliferates.

O You who casts Your light deep in their breasts,
Guide us to their lights, make them manifest.

La Ila Ha Illallah!

Sing it with sincere ardour!
Drink it in with cheer and fervour!
The authentic formula!
La ilaha illallah!

Hear it echo in your dreams!
Wear this credo with esteem!
It's the manifesto supreme!
La ilaha illallah!

Through it strengthens certainty!
View it with sincerity!
Imbue it, oh humanity!
La ilaha illallah!

In the great glory of dawn
When dusk's canopy is drawn
Read it happily, feel reborn!
La ilaha illallah!

Hidden in it lies relief,
Medicine for spiritual diseases,
It's the divine remedy!
La ilaha illallah!

Light of Unity appear
In those ones who persevere
Reciting with strong candour!
La ilaha illallah!

Peace and blessings on the one,
Prayers upon the noble one,

Who brought us the Kalima!
La ilaha illallah!

Poetic Prayers

Help me in my desperate plight, O Lord,
The world is wrestling with my heart, O Lord,
Dragging me down an abyss, O Lord,
Desiring to suppress my light, O Lord,
So rescue me from my poor plight, My Dear Lord.

A voice is striving to deceive, O Lord,
Persuading me that I exist, O Lord,
Independent of Your act, O Lord,
A random, floating speck of dust, O Lord
So strengthen me in Your knowledge, My Dear Lord.

The world urges me to idolise, O Lord,
The gods of wealth and happiness, O Lord,
And serve the goddesses of thrills, O Lord,
Until the world means everything, O Lord,
So make my true desire You, My Dear Lord.

I'm lost and I am wandering, O Lord,
I'm covered in the dust of sin, O Lord,
Forgive me for my shortcomings, O Lord.
Show me the dawning of Your Light, O Lord.
Extinguish all my worldly fears, O Lord,
Give me strength to hold my reins, O Lord,
Prepare me for my coming death, O Lord,
Protect me from complacency, O Lord,
Enshroud my sadness with some cheer, O Lord,
Pluck me out of selfish states, My dear, Lord.

I ask you for Your special help, O Lord,
You made me, my return's to You, O Lord,
You are my creator and my Friend, O Lord,

You gave me life and will bring me death, O Lord,
I ask you through the sanctity, O Lord
Of the jewel of humanity, O Lord
The mirror of divinity, O Lord,
Forgive me and my community, My dear Lord.

And peace and blessings on that very one, O Lord,
Whose face brought longing tears out from the sun, My
Dear Lord.

Poetic Prayers

O Allah!
Lord of the brightest mornings
and the darkest nights!
Lord of our terrible times
and the moments of our greatest delights!
O Allah!
Protect us in these dark days
of murder and strife
Wrap us in Your love,
with Your cloak of security and might!
Surround us with Your
impenetrable forces of light.
Repel and expel all destructive forces
that seek to infiltrate
Our homes, our streets, our neighbourhoods
and inner states.
O Allah Most High!
Though we stand tall,
we are nothing but a tribe of ants
And this world is a hungry heron,
pecking, constantly on the attack
We are in dire need of Your help,
so enshroud our innate fragility,
Without You, we have no hope
of overcoming difficulty,
Be with us always, O Lord,
in times of ease and adversity.

The Path to the Mosque

The path to the mosque is tough, takes longer
The hazards great, filled with hidden dangers.
On one side, the path ascends high, to the right
But another drops dangerously down, to the left.
The path to the right is steep and thin
One needs balance to remain therein
Keeping aground needs patience and time
Strength is required to follow this line.
The path to the left is open and wide
Movement is easy, a bicycle ride!
One can thoughtlessly follow it down
Whistling tunes, relaxing around.
Pray, bravely take the path to right
As when one finally reaches the mosque
It feels like a palace of paradise.
One feels like a hardened traveller
Having wondered over perilous places
Eternally searching and moving
Then finally finding friendly faces!
But the path to the left makes your mind wonder
The ease of it makes you linger
around the comfort, and you're not bothered to seek
Perhaps visiting the mosque hardly once a week...
The path to the right may seem too hazardous to face,
But it's the only road, where we will find His Grace.

For Our Mothers and Fathers

For Our Fathers

Like a roof, giving shelter from the cold,
Like foundations, shouldering the weight of his household,
Like a candle, lighting up his family's world,
Like cement, binding us together with a firm hold,
is our father

And as our father matures in years and wisdom
Like a fruit tree, firmly rooted in the garden
Though the branches seem to wither and weaken
Still the fruits appear and grow and drop and ripen
from our father

O Lord, bless our father immensely and endlessly
For his hard work, for his guidance and generosity
Help us to benefit from the fruit of his efforts and wisdom
Accept these sincere prayers from grateful and loving
children
for our father.

For Our Mothers

Like the fire, giving warmth and glowing so bright
Like the water, showering her family with life
Like a fur blanket, comforting with sheer delight
Like medicine, soothing our troubles and strife
is our mother.

And as we grow in strength and venture out of the nest
And find other loves, pursuing our own projects
Still her heart aches with an emptiness

For the love of God dwells in her breast
in our mother

O Lord, bless our mother without end
for her love, on which our sorry lives depend
Help us to gladden her, and her needs we attend
Keep a special place for our loving friend,
for our mother.

Seeking Knowledge

All knowledge worth seeking
is like a never-ending dining table
covered with wholesome food.
Some stand gobbling wantonly
Wanting everything at once
While others only nibble
Their taste buds hardly aroused.
Pray let us sit at the table
With attention to manners and grace
Then let us dine with peace and patience
So we can enjoy the full measure of the taste.

The Weeping Man I Met Around The Kaaba

There was this personage
whom I met at the pilgrimage
whose holy tears I will never forget.
Profusely they were shed
falling without relenting
while we orbited the House of God.
Dressed in ihram,
the hajjis made tawaaf
like a flowing ring of light.
This moment had played
in my mind for nights and days
I marvelled at the possibilities.
What would I see?
How would I feel?
In the footsteps of Anbiya.
Would I feel free?
And sense the reality?
Would Allah accept my pilgrimage?
But when the moment arrived
to my complete surprise
I wasn't moved as I hoped to be.
Instead I was dry
no tears touched my eyes,
I marched, whispering empty prayers.
Full of sheer grief,
how could I be so cheap!?
distracted and stonehearted!
My heavy heart
screamed out in alarm
I should be shedding bitter tears,
for my sins
here in the kernel,

my tears could win me heaven.
Then I looked
closely and shook
and saw a wondrous sight.
This man's eyes
tears falling, brimming with light
sobbing as he made his rounds.
He didn't stop
as he made tawaf
the tears soaked through his beard.
And my heart
shook and broke into parts
when confronted with such true feeling.
I was curious
to find out who he was
and why he cried for himself.
When I touched
his shoulder, he looked up
his eyes shone twinkling and luminous.
Then his reply
to my attempt to pry
left me bewildered, mystified.
He said, "I cry
with tears filling my eyes
I try but they just don't stop.
Because I pray
for all Muslims on this special day
Allah save them from the fire and dismay.
Forgive their sins
and their shortcomings
admit them into Paradise."
I stepped back
shocked and taken aback
were my ears hearing correctly?
This lonely man
not for his own demands

but for the sins of man he shed his tears.

When I Tasted Their Tears

When I tasted their tears
my heart never recovered
I felt the love that touched their souls
that moved these blessed brothers.

When I first witnessed their adulation
at the grave of Al Hussain
My head swelled up with sheer outrage
Did they feel no shame?

Sobbing like a bunch of women!
Embracing idolatry!
Calling out to one who can not answer,
What confounded stupidity!

They sang, they prayed, with pious display
They cried, they even danced!
I think they're probably Shia nuts
They'd beat themselves given a chance!

What on earth are they crying for?
They should cry for their own sins!
No wonder the Muslim world's a mess
Chasing innovations and chasing whims!
My hands itched for some bold action
I must change this with my hand
I disappeared down the nearest alley
Returned with a grenade hidden in my hand.

I would teach these innovators how
misguided their tears were
the fire of hell would destroy them all

the spectre of idolatry would burn.

I was just about to release the pin
Throw it in and run away
Then from a distance watch the sight
of falsehood in dismay.

When one of these misguided men
Looked me straight in the eye
His glance pierced something deep within
And I could not help but cry.

Suddenly, within my heart
I felt it heating up
The flame of love had been ignited
And now my spirit would erupt!

With the grenade still in my pocket
I collapsed and sobbed and wailed
For there and then I heard a voice,
As if it was Al Hussain!

No one there could console me
As the tears shook me and just shook
I tried to give my mind a chance
but love, it overtook!

And now I have tasted their tears
My tears just will not end
The fire of the love of God
Has made me its dear friend.

So listen to my story friend
Before you ever try
And ridicule the tears of men
Who yearn for those who've died.

For they are not dead at all
Their spirits live so free
And now the tears give no respite
The fire of love has consumed me!

Note:
This poem was inspired by the brothers, Abo Shar,
who recorded their visitation of the shrine of Imam Al
Hussain in Cairo. May Allah sanctify his secret.

Not My Business

"So long as they don't take the yam from my savouring mouth."
Niyi Osundare

They firebombed the tomb of Al Rifai
All that remained was mounds of rubbles in piles,
But what business is it to me and to my ilk?
As long as they've purged the bida and shirk.

They drove out the Yazidis and Christians
Chased them out in their thousands and millions
But what business is it to me and to my ilk?
As long as they have purged the bida and shirk.

They blocked the roads and set up their own courts
Banning all sinful goods and useless sports
But what business is it to me and to my ilk?
As long as they have purged the bida and shirk.

They censured and pursued any woman or girl
Without niqaab, their face bare to the world,
But what business is it to me and to my ilk,
As long as they have purged the bida and shirk.

But one day they knocked upon my door
Grabbing me and dragging me to the floor
Demanding me to give to them my life
One of them fancied my only daughter for a second wife.
And when they took her from me and my ilk,
I found that in them lived a subtle hidden shirk.

Seven Nufus Were On The Loose

Seven nufus were on the loose
One day from Ramadan
They met in Sousse for some couscous
Before the maghrib azaan.

The first, a rioter, the sin-inciter,
The crazy imp, Ammara.
The second ilk, ridden with guilt,
Reproachful soul, Lowwaama.
The third, on fire, with love inspired
The stirring one, Mulhama.
The fourth, serene, like mountain streams,
The earnest, Mutmainna.
The fifth, contented, with perfume scented,
The honourable, Raadiyya.
The sixth, found-pleasing, the love unceasing,
The gracious one, Mardiyya.
The seventh, perfect, from the elect,
The wondrous, Kamila.

As they met and sat then began their chat,
Awaiting their great couscous,
Ammara cursed like the devil's nurse
His face twisted with disgust:

"This Ramadan; it does me harm,
I really can't be bothered!
One whole month, down in the dumps,
Pleasures are banned; O brother!"

"I'll try my best to pass this test,"
Lamented poor Lowwaama,

"I find it hard to stay on guard
I wish I was a llama!"

"I can not wait to taste a date
At the end of each day's fasting
A blessed time will here arrive,"
Mulhama said, forecasting.

"Enjoy the food, enjoy the mood,"
Exulted Mutmainna,
"Be pleased with fasting, grace everlasting
Purifying the sinner."

"I am contented with this unprecedented
Occurrence of Divine favour
Each year unique, with special mystique
I love Ramadan," Said Raadiyya.

"I am most pleased with His decrees,"
Celebrated Mardiyya,
"We are so blessed, with Ramadan our guest
It's sustenance from our Sharia."

"Come join me brothers! Let's rediscover
Our origins in Ramadan,
We're nothing but meanings, which is He conceiving,"
Said Kamila, so captivating and so calm.

"Don't give me drama!" argued Ammara
"I ain't missing out this month, mate!
X-Men will be on, the Euros are on
And a girl has asked me out on a date!
You keep up your fasting, I'll keep flabbergasting
the ladies with my exhilaration
I ain't got the time for things so sublime
Ramadan is a scourge on my reputation!"

Lowwama got haughty: "you are such a naughty!
Haven't you got any shame?
I don't find it easy; I find fasting queasy
But I'll still have a go all the same."

A smile had arrived upon the other five
Who sat eating their couscous so gently
"Ammara, we'll guide you, Lowwama we'll help you
Ramadan will fill you with plenty.
If you listen to us; follow without a fuss
Allah will make you His familiar
In just a brief moment, His works are so potent,
Ammara can become Kamila.
We are seven nufus, we're all on the loose
And our gathering here was intentional
The prince and the pauper, the sinner and scholar
Ramadan equalises our potential.
We are seven positions, in the Quran we are mentioned,
The seven degrees of the soul
Allah bless Al Shabrawi, wise as the Kalahari,
The author, the crown of the poles."

Notes:
This poem was influenced by the following work:
Degrees of the Soul by Shaykh Abdul Khaliq Al
Shabrawi, translated by Dr Mostafa Al Badawi.

How Can You Love Muhammad So Much?

How can you love Muhammad so much?
How can you show such devotion?
What do you see in this Arabian?
Why does he stir your emotions?
All we have heard is his harem of wives
Included the little girl Aisha
We hear of his call for Islamic jihad
And his Quran so hard to decipher.
How can we not love Muhammad so much?
How can we not just adore him?
How can we not share his wonderful stories?
How can our yearning ignore him?
All we have heard from our mothers and fathers
Our grandparents and also our scholars
Is how the light shone when he smiled and he wept
And how he showed poor people honour.
All we have read in our vast holy books
And the publications in our studies
Is how he would wake in the dead of the night
And pray with all his heart and his body.
All that we know is his soul is a light
The secret of heavenly mercy
He met with a smile and despite all his trials
He even showed animals such courtesy
How can we not love his reality?
When he manifests in our true dreams
We see his broad face and the mystical grace
We awaken with tears so serene.
How can you see what we ourselves see?
When all that you see is your perception
You see a phantom of your imaginations
But we see a man of sincere intentions

We see a man who inspires us
Who makes us strive for perfection
We see a man who fascinates us
Who makes us apply self-correction
We see a man who fills us with love
For mankind and for all of nature
So how can we not love Muhammad so much?
When we have been smitten by his stature.
You can remain in your ivory towers
Of civilisational hubris
Sinking in pits of cynical bliss
Embracing your mind's incubus
We will persist in the sheer bliss
Of loving our Prophet Muhammad
Let haters hate and consume folly's bait
Let lovers live with their beloved.

I'll Never Forget The Time I Went To Shaam

I'll never forget the time I went to Shaam
Emerging stood the beating heart, Damascus,
Multitudes of minarets, like a sea of candles
Domes of various sizes and stunning hues
The mountains glistened behind, enhancing the view
I'll never forget the time I went to Shaam
Shaykh Tanweer and the band of intrepid students
They smiled and laughed, leading us through the streets
A world of light and mystery lay before us
A world of God's people spread before us
Entranced with wonder
We stepped into Souk Hammadiyah
Colours twinkled under the snaking iron arches
The scent of rich baklava and flowing oud
Traders spoke in animated moods
We glided through arriving into the courtyard
The city's essence, masjid Al Ummawi
The courtyard filled with children buzzing and giggling
I'll never forget the time I went to Shaam
Inside the mosque, echoes reverberated
Blessed souls chanting verse of Quran
Nabi Yahya's resting place enlightened the hall
We prayed and whispered, completely enthralled
Then a man tooks us to an office
Reposing there was Shaykh Abdul Razzaq Al Halabi
It seemed that he was drenched in divine light
When he gazed at us, it felt he gazed into our souls
Then, outside, who should be walking along the street
None other than Shaykh Ramadan Al Buti
He shook our hands as if we were his friends
I'll never forget the time I went to Shaam
We scaled the scorching, rising, ancient streets

Heading for the tomb of Shaykh Al Akbar
Strange his resting place was near the mountains
Like a wondrous jewel hidden beneath the rocks
Unseen lights surrounded Salihiyya
The sun's rays enshrouded the paths
Suddenly Shaykhs and dervishes appeared
We stumbled upon the gathering Salat Ala Nabi
The devotees rocked and swayed in remembrance
Their voices for Allah took our breaths away
I'll never forget the time I went to Shaam
We entered into the realm of Shaykh Shaghouri
He was so old, but his soul glowed like the moon
Although we were a group of heedless Brits
He took our hands and kissed them like we were it!
Then up and up upon Jabal Qasioun
We entered the cave where the mountain wept for blood
Upon the slopes there stood a weathering masjid
The meeting place of the saints, Al Arbaeen
In the hall we saw these enigmatic mihrabs
Each one signifying one of the abdaal
The imam with orange beard greeted us with glee
What a profound place this seemed to be.
Down we came upon a crazy Suzuki
Rocketting down the streets like a roller coaster
To this day, I reckon that the driver
Believed that he was something like Schumacher!
I'll never forget the time I went to Shaam
May Allah spread His peace upon Bilaad Ash Shaam
For the sake of Al Mustafa, protect Bilaad Ash Shaam

ABOUT THE AUTHOR

Novid Shaid is an English teacher from the UK, who has taught in various secondary schools for over fifteen years. His first published work is the mystical thriller novel: *The Hidden Ones*, which is available on Amazon. He has also published *Short Stories* and a book of poetry called *The Prophet's Time In Rhyme*.

23935726R00067

Printed in Great Britain
by Amazon